Watching the Seasons

Summer

by Emily C. Dawson

Bullfrog Books

Ideas for Parents and Teachers

Bullfrog Books let children practice nonfiction reading at the earliest reading levels. Repetition, familiar words, and photo labels support early readers. Here are some tips for reading with children.

Before Reading
- Discuss the cover photo. What does it tell them?

- Look at the picture glossary together. Read and discuss the words.

Read the Book
- "Walk" through the book and look at the photos. Let the child ask questions. Point out the photo labels.

- Read the book to the child, or have him or her read independently.

After Reading
- Prompt the child to think more. Ask: What is summer like where you live? What do you like to do in summer?

Bullfrog Books are published by Jump!
5357 Penn Avenue South, Minneapolis, MN 55419
www.jumplibrary.com

Library of Congress Cataloging-in-Publication Data
Dawson, Emily C.
Summer / by Emily C. Dawson.
   p. cm. — (Watching the seasons) (Bullfrog books)
Summary: "This photo-illustrated book for early readers describes how summer weather affects the actions of animals, the growth of plants, and the activities of people. Includes photo glossary" —Provided by publisher.
Includes bibliographical references and index.
Audience: Grades K-3.
ISBN 978-1-62031-015-1 (hbk.)
1. Summer—Juvenile literature. I. Title.
QB637.6.D378 2013
508.2--dc23
                                        2012009115

Series Editor: Rebecca Glaser
Series Designer: Ellen Huber
Photo Researcher: Heather Dreisbach

Photo Credits
Dreamstime, 4, 16, 23tl; Getty Images, 15, 18-19, 21; Shutterstock, 2b, 2t, 8, 8-9, 10, 11, 14, 16-17, 22, 23bl, 19, 20, 23tr, 24; SuperStock, 5, 6-7, 12

Printed in the United States of America at Corporate Graphics, in North Mankato, Minnesota.
7-2012 / 1124
10 9 8 7 6 5 4 3 2 1

Table of Contents

Summer Days

In summer, days are long.

The sun sets late.

5

In summer, animals grow up.

Loons teach their babies to fish.

In summer,
spiders spin.

A silky web
traps bugs.

A spider saves
the bug to eat
later.

web

In summer, plants grow.

Watermelon is ready to eat. Yum!

In summer, trees
grow leaves.

They make shade.

Jen stays cool
in the shade.

In summer,
it is hot.

Meg drinks ice-cold
lemonade. Ahh!

14

hail

In summer, clouds thunder.
Lightning flashes. It rains.
Sometimes it hails!

In summer, kids play.
Abdi plays T-ball.
John swims at
the lake.

In summer, people camp.

Eve sleeps in a tent.

What do you do in summer?

Watching the Seasons

Spring

Summer

Winter

Fall

Picture Glossary

hail
Small bits of ice that fall from the sky like rain.

loon
A large bird with webbed feet that dives for food.

lightning
A flash of light in the sky when electricity moves in the clouds.

shade
A place that is sheltered from sunlight.

Index

To Learn More

Learning more is as easy as 1, 2, 3.

1) Go to www.factsurfer.com

2) Enter "summer" into the search box.

3) Click the "Surf" button to see a list of websites.

With factsurfer.com, finding more information is just a click away.